This book is dedicated to all who find Nature

not an adversary to conquer and destroy, but a storehouse

of infinite knowledge and experience linking man to

all things past and present. They know conserving the natural

environment is essential to our future well-being.

DEATH VALLEY
THE STORY BEHIND THE SCENERY®

by Bill Clark

Bill Clark is a retired park ranger. A graduate in geology from Tufts University, Bill served several years in Death Valley. He wrote the original *Death Valley: The Story Behind the Scenery* in 1972 and has updated it several times. He tells the story of this often maligned desert, revealing in intimate detail its true essence—its subtle beauties, spectacular forms, and surprising variety.

Death Valley National Park, *in eastern California and western Nevada, was first set aside in 1933 to preserve this unique desert that includes the lowest point in the Western Hemisphere.*

Front cover: The Panamints, Manly Beacon, and the valley floor; photo by Tom Algire. Inside front cover: Panamint Range with desert sunflowers; photo by Larry Ulrich. Page 1: Desert mariposa; photo by Fred Hirschmann. Pages 2/3: Ripple-patterned dunes at Mesquite Flat; photo by Jeff Gnass.

Edited by Cheri C. Madison. Book design by K. C. DenDooven.

Fourteenth Printing, Revised Edition• 2005

DEATH VALLEY: THE STORY BEHIND THE SCENERY. © 2002 KC PUBLICATIONS, INC.
"*The Story Behind the Scenery*"; *the Eagle / Flag icon on Front Cover are registered in the U.S. Patent and Trademark Office.*
LC 2001096581. ISBN 0-88714-235-4.

*T*he flowing sand expresses the desert wind in infinite patterns—
always the same, always changing. Today's contours are
sharp—and gentle. Light and shadow follow one another,

sunrise to sunset. Today's beauty is the same tomorrow, and different. The dunes are an ephemeral and infinite art form. The Sand Dunes are eternally becoming . . .

JEFF GNASS

Death Valley lies between the high cold Great Basin Desert to the north and the warmer Mojave Desert to the south. It is a wonderland far different from the barren, blistered land evoked by the name Death Valley.

Death Valley is part of the Great Basin—that part of the intermountain West that is cut off from the sea—and the geological Basin and Range Province—the almost endless repetition of block faulted valleys and mountains between California and Utah.

Death Valley is beauty and excitement. Every year it calls tens of thousands of visitors to explore North America's lowest and hottest place, the roads and trails, the mountains and the great alluvial fans, and Scotty's Castle—perhaps the most unexpected and unreal feature in this vast land of almost infinite variety.

All of Death Valley is below Dantes View—not an imagined Purgatory, but a desert wonderland for all to enjoy. The Black Mountains in the foreground and the Panamints on the opposite side enclose the deepest part of the valley.

The Death Valley Story

Over a century ago, a young advertising manager for a borax company came to Death Valley. Because of his love for the outdoors, Steve Mather traded business for government, and in 1916 became the first director of the National Park Service. He was among the first to recognize that:

Death Valley is space—5,000 square miles. The valley is 150 miles long. From the lowest place near Badwater (282 feet below sea level) to the top of Telescope Peak (11,049 feet above sea level), the vertical relief is over two miles.

Death Valley is color—Blinding white salt, yellow mud, rocks of every color—black, green, orange, brown—evergreen forest, white snow, and blue sky.

Death Valley is life—Creosote bush and desert holly and "belly flowers," the pupfish and the bighorn, kangaroo rats and coyotes, roadrunners and the colorful birds that flock to the Furnace Creek oasis, and golden eagles.

Death Valley is weather—Most people come in the fall and winter, when Death Valley's weather is just about perfect for whatever you want to do. More and more are coming in summer to experience the hottest place—temperatures often over 120° F—and loving it!

Death Valley is variety—Saltpan and mountain, alluvial fan and sheer-walled canyon, playa and volcanic crater, and—most unbelievable of all—Scotty's Castle.

Death Valley is excitement—Visitors in this desert find steep canyon walls, historic mines, mountain roads, bicycling, hiking, photography. And . . .

Death Valley is peace—Watching the silence of light and shadow following the sun across the space—and hearing the silence of moonlight flooding the space with silver.

JOHN ELK III

Mosaic Canyon beckons the hiker to pass into the deeper, wilder Death Valley. Mud and rocks on the canyon floor are as recent as the last rain. Canyon walls are blocks of mountain tumbled down as the valley was created, and cemented into the mosaic. The blocks are ancient dolomite, formed on the shallow edge of the Pacific Ocean.

Sand Dunes–Mountain
ranges weather and erode,
and sand grains are a byproduct. Strong winds sweep the sand along the valley floor. Near
Stovepipe Wells the Valley widens and the south wind slows–losing its power to sweep the tiny
grains. The North wind breaks into eddies around Tucki Mountain, dropping it's sand here.

Basin and range
faulting built
the mountain
wall—two miles
high to the top
of the Panamints. Huge
alluvial fans are the
mud, sand, and rock
that was mountain.
Heat and wind
evaporate the water
and leave the saltpan
on the valley floor.

*Death Valley has higher temperatures
and less rainfall than any place in North America.
Heat and drought affect everything—
plant and animal, rock and water. Those who visit
are treated to desert beyond imagination.*

The Hottest Place

Death Valley is hot—the average high temperature in July is 116° F; the average low is 88° F. The coolest month is January, with an average high of 65°F and an average low of 29° F. In the course of a year, temperatures on the valley floor vary by more than 100° F. At any one time, the temperature difference between Telescope Peak (11,049 feet) and Furnace Creek (-192 feet) may be over 50° F.

Death Valley's average yearly rainfall is less than 2 inches. The potential evaporation—150 inches per year—far exceeds the actual rainfall. Coastal areas of California receive only 10 or 15 inches of rain per year. With the rain shadow of the Sierra Nevada standing between Death Valley and the Pacific Ocean, it is small wonder that the valley is so parched.

In summer, rising hot air reinforces aridity in two ways: (1) Locally, rising hot air is replaced by heavier cool air flowing down off the mountains—but the cooler mountain air is heated by compression as it descends. (2) Regionally, hot air rises over the southwestern deserts, creating a low-pressure system with counterclockwise circulation that pumps hot, dry air north from the Mexican Plateau. Occasional thunderstorms result when moist air is drawn into the system from either the Pacific Ocean or the Gulf of Mexico—spectacular nighttime light-shows over the mountain barriers.

From November through March, Death Valley is blessed with moderate temperatures, cloudless days, and clear air. Occasional winter storms bring life-giving rain.

TOM GAMACHE

RUSS FINLEY

Salt grass can tolerate soils with a greater salt concentration than the oceans. Summer heat and evaporation increase the concentration of salt, testing the strength of salt grass to survive on the edge of the saltpan. Rains wash mud and sand, salts and other minerals onto the valley floor. Most of the water evaporates. The saltpan is continually replenished.

The parched, cracked earth is a lake bed—actually a lake only during and just after the infrequent rain. Desert holly is a saltbush—tolerant of salt and drought. After a rain, muddy water finds its way to the lowest places. The edge of the dry lake bed—the playa—is a favored location, just above the salty muds.

The generally arid climate of the southwest, the thermal low pressure system, the Sierra Nevadan rain shadow, and the dimensions of the valley all combine to make Death Valley the hottest and driest place in North America.

LANDFORMS IN THE HOTTEST PLACE

Death Valley has the distinctive landforms common to deserts around the world. Nearly barren mountains tower over huge alluvial fans. Some of the canyons have barely scratched the mountain walls. There is a tree line at about 6,000 feet, below which few trees can survive. At lower elevations,

FRED HIRSCHMANN

gravels and muds are carved into badlands. Surface water evaporates in the closed basins, leaving salts, borates, and other water-soluble minerals—and forming salt-encrusted salinas. Yellow muds washed off surrounding mountains by the infrequent rains form playas such as The Racetrack.

Wind sweeps unhindered across the valley, piling sand in favored locations and carrying dust miles into the air. All but the most gentle rains produce sheetflooding, washing out roads in some places, burying them under tons of rock and mud in others. Each rain moves a thousand, or a million, tons of sand and mud and rock a little farther downslope. Above the buried bedrock floor of Death Valley is perhaps 9,000 feet of mud, sand, and salt washed out of the mountains—filling the valley almost to sea level.

Ridges are knife edged. Canyons walls are steep. Poorly cemented conglomerates (pebbles, sand, and mud) stand erect in vertical walls rising a hundred feet and more. The hard-rock limestone walls of Titus Canyon and Lost Burro Gap stand in near vertical cliffs a thousand feet high.

Desert varnish—a shiny black iron and manganese oxide—covers many rock surfaces. The wind removes sand and silt from around and beneath cobbles, and rotates them until they fit together as tight as the pieces of a mosaic. The resulting desert pavement is often covered with desert varnish, gleaming like a broken mirror in the sun.

The lack of vegetation permits the wind to gather sand into dunes. Near Stovepipe Wells, the widening of the valley reduces the velocity of the wind—and the wind gathers the sand.

Death Valley's badlands—the yellow muds of Furnace Creek Wash—are the result of climate and mineralogy. In the dry climate there is little vegetation to capture rainfall. Plate-shaped clay minerals in the mud deflect the rain, preventing it from soaking into the ground. The water flows across the surface of the mud, carving it into badlands.

"Water, water, everywhere. Nor any drop to drink," lamented Samuel Taylor Coleridge in "The Rhyme of the Ancient Mariner." The lament applies in Death Valley. Not snow, but salt, coats the surface with white. Salt Creek, aptly named, flows from the Sand Dunes south into the saltpan. Evaporation at the surface wicks up the salt-saturated water from beneath the ground. At the surface the water evaporates, leaving even more salt behind. Pickleweed, growing on the small Salt Creek islands, is a phreatophyte—a plant needing a constant supply of water. It can live in soil containing up to six percent salt.

K. C. DENDOOVEN

By full moon Death Valley *is enchanting and bizarre, a surreal wonderland. At Zabriskie Point, sterile yellow muds erode into steep-walled gullies—badlands— the combination of drought and clay minerals in the mud. The clay minerals are flat and plate shaped— they keep the infrequent rainfall on the surface, where it expends all of its downhill energy carving the mud.*

"Ridges are
KNIFE
EDGED.
Canyon walls
are
steep…"

LIFE IN THE HOTTEST PLACE

Death Valley's life is diverse. The desert plants have adapted to the scant rainfall and brutal evaporation. Most desert plants have evolved means of conserving water, once they get it. Creosote bush has a resinous coating on its leaves. The trunk of a cactus

is a water barrel. The spines of cactus conserve water by providing a cushion of still air around the plant, protecting it from the desiccating winds.

Many of Death Valley's plants have active life for only a small portion of the year. For some, the proper combination of rainfall and temperature triggers growth; others may require the same combination, but within a particular season. Many seeds have growth inhibitors, which are washed off by sufficient rainfall. Correct temperatures activate a growth-inducing enzyme, and active life begins. Within the few weeks of their life spans, they germinate, grow, produce flowers and then seeds, and die. Some seeds always remain dormant, ensuring that there will always be a next generation. Occasionally,

rainfall and temperature combine to produce truly spectacular spring wildflower displays.

The plants are the base for the pyramid of life. In a simplistic example: a thousand pounds of mesquite beans might support a hundred pounds of kangaroo rat, food in turn for ten pounds of sidewinder, perhaps sufficient food for one pound of red-tailed hawk. This progression is a food chain—real life is never so simple. The more accurate picture is a web of life—most animals have alternate food supplies. Coyotes eat many kinds of rodents and lizards, and even dates from the grove at Furnace Creek. Some lizards are vegetarians, some are omnivores, others eat only smaller lizards. But there must always be a surplus. Some kangaroo rats must evade the hunters and raise their offspring successfully. Grazing animals must not crop their food to the ground.

BIGHORN IN THE HOTTEST PLACE

Desert bighorn are superbly adapted. They are good conservationists. Nervous browsers, they are continually in motion. Instead of stripping the cover and then moving on, they eat only a little—about two percent of the food available in any one area—and move on. One herd might range over an area 20 miles in diameter.

In winter they require little water. Thirst is satisfied with the moisture contained in their food. In the hottest part of summer they usually require water once every three days. Greater water requirements would confine them to a smaller range and increase their impact on the fragile desert.

In the past they had to contend with hunters, human appropriation of water sources, and feral burros. Bighorn are shy—the increasing numbers of vehicles on backcountry roads drive them further back into the mountains, reducing their range.

In the 20th century, the major threat to the bighorn was from burros. The years around 1900

Death Valley is dry—but there are infrequent rains. In the desert, water can produce strange effects—in this case "skating" rocks. The Racetrack is a playa—an intermittent lake bed—in northern Death Valley. Playas are among the world's flattest surfaces and, after a rain, among the most slippery. At The Racetrack, rocks occasionally tumble off the surrounding mountains onto the lake bed. Then, after a rain, strong gusty winds raft the boulders across the wet, slippery mud—leaving their trails behind them. The same winds can pile up the water, less than an inch deep, onto one side of the playa. The pattern of the mud cracks is typical of playa surfaces, resulting from contraction of the muds as they dry.

DENNIS FLAHERTY

Because of its scarcity, the work *of water is more easily seen in the desert. Here the effect is magnified into a cascading stream of desert sunflowers. Water, running downhill, carves a shallow gully. The gully collects runoff from the higher land to the sides. The extra water produces this profusion of yellow and green. In a desert, drought follows rain, so the seeds produced by these flowers will not germinate right away, even though there might be moisture and reasonable air temperatures. The seeds will remain dormant until a growth inhibitor is washed off them the following year—or the next.*

DENNIS FLAHERTY

The Devils Cornfield is named for its arrowweed "cornshocks." Arrowweed thrives where the groundwater is only slightly salty—about one percent. Devils Cornfield is in the northern part of the Salt Creek drainage, near the Sand Dunes. Devils Cornfield is one of many Death Valley place names having to do with the devil or death—Funeral Mountains, Coffin Peak, Devils Golf Course, Dantes View (of Purgatory). When places in Death Valley were being named, wilderness was to be conquered and tamed. Death Valley place names may well reflect fears felt by people facing unconquerable wilderness. What names would we give these places if we were seeing them for the first time today?

because, in a national park or monument, the needs of the native animals take precedence over those of exotic (introduced) species. A few feral animals probably wander in, but now there are probably less than 200 burros in Death Valley at any one time—and about 2,000 bighorn.

Death Valley is wild and big. Its web of life is broad and diverse. Restoring and maintaining the delicate balance that allows over 1,300 native plant and animal species to live here is one of the major undertakings of the National Park Service.

were the heyday of the "single-blanket jackass prospector." Some of the prospectors' burros escaped or were turned loose. By the 1970s the fragile Death Valley ecosystem supported thousands of burros—at the expense of native plants and animals—and the burro population was increasing. Water sources were fouled, and large areas of the park were overgrazed.

Finally a beginning was made toward restoring the natural desert. Between 1983 and 1987 over 6,000 burros, 87 horses, and 4 mules were live trapped and removed from the park. The burros were removed

DEATH VALLEY EXPEDITION—1891

The study of the natural history of Death Valley began with the 1891 Death Valley Expedition. Members included famous names in the birth of the ecology movement in this country: Frederick Vernon Colville, C. Hart Merriam, George Bird Grinnell, T. S. Palmer, and Vernon Bailey.

The botany study of Death Valley began with Colville's *Botany of the Death Valley Expedition*. Merriam was to have written a companion volume on the people and animals of the valley—if this was actually written, it has since been lost.

DAVID MUENCH

The Devils Golf Course is a heck of a place to lose a golf ball. The massive rock salt—three to five feet deep— was deposited when a shallow salty lake covering the floor of Death Valley dried up about 2,000 years ago. In yet another example of the power of water in the desert, wind-driven rain dissolves the salt into the jagged pinnacles seen today.

Colville's work stands as a classic in field ecology. He made detailed studies of the principles of plant distribution, the actual distribution of the plants of the eastern California deserts, and the characteristics and adaptations that allow these plants to live in this desert. Over 2,000 specimens were collected, over 1,200 species and varieties were described, and 42 plants previously unknown were reported for the first time.

SUGGESTED READING

COOK, KAYCI. *in pictures Death Valley: The Continuing Story*. Las Vegas, NV: KC Publications, Inc., 1989.

FERRIS, ROXANNA S. *Death Valley Wildflowers*. Bishop, CA: Death Valley Natural History Assn., 1983.

HIRSCHMANN, FRED & RANDI. Environmental History by Mark A. Schlenz. *Death Valley National Park*. Santa Barbara, CA: Companion Press, 1988.

STEWART, JON MARK. *Mojave Desert Wildflowers*. Albuquerque, NM: Jon Stewart Photography, 1998.

Watch a coyote trotting slowly across the desert floor. He is home— knowing how and where to find food and water. Or a sidewinder looping across the desert sand— he, too, is home.

Seeing Life in the Valley

BILL RATCLIFFE

DAVID MUENCH

Death Valley sage clings to life on a barren canyon wall. Almost all of the precious rainwater bounces off the rocks and is lost. But the roots reach deep into the cracks, where the precious water gathers and is protected from sun and wind—and evaporation.

The beavertail cactus's shallow roots catch the infrequent rains and store the water in its fleshy stems. The brilliant flowers are an indication of the valley's insect life.

Plants of Death Valley

Over 900 plant species are spread out over 5,000 square miles of wild land from below sea level to two miles above. Four major plant zones are determined by elevation:

The *Lower Sonoran Zone* occupies the lowest 4,000 feet. Desert holly and creosote bush dominate alluvial fans, and plant density increases with increasing elevation—at 1,000 feet there are twice as many plants as at sea level. Also with increasing elevation, sagebrush and other desert shrubs become more common.

Piñon pine and juniper identify the *Upper Sonoran Zone*, 4,000 to about 8,500 feet, where it gives way to the *Transition Zone* with Sierra juniper and mountain mahogany. Above 9,000 feet is the *Subalpine Zone* with limber and bristlecone pines.

Creosote bush has a wide shallow root system. The shrubs appear to be carefully spaced to avoid competition for water. In fact, the spacing is because each plant secretes a poison that prevents new plants from growing in its territory.

Rare & Unique in Death Valley

Because of the extreme climate and extreme topography, some plants live only in Death Valley. Others are extremely rare, limited to favored locations.

Death Valley milkvetch, with its unique purple color.

Death Valley monkeyflower often grows in limestone crevasses.

Panamint daisies thrive in only a few rocky washes. It is not a widespread plant.

Eureka Dunes evening primrose, found only on these dunes.

Animals of Death Valley

Water is the key to life. Because water is plentiful, there are probably more wild plants and animals at Furnace Creek than any other place in the park. Coyotes and roadrunners are common sights at Scotty's Castle and around the Death Valley Museum. Furnace Creek is a popular stop for migratory birds.

Mesquite groves are popular areas to seek desert wildlife—where mesquite beans support a population of kangaroo rats and other rodents—prey for sidewinders and coyotes.

The evergreen forest of the Panamint Mountains has water—and is home for several rare species of salamanders.

The lowest part of the saltpan is the only Death Valley environment too harsh for life. Algae and pupfish live in salt pools around the edges of the saltpan.

Feeding on snakes, lizards, and insects, the roadrunner is superbly adapted to the southwest desert—and to the works of people. This one posed at Scotty's Castle. Surprise—the roadrunner is a member of the cuckoo family.

Desert tortoises are vegetarians, spending a lot of time hibernating while waiting for the next crop.

Coyotes have their own adaptations for life in the desert. First, they are omnivores, eating almost anything and everything. Second, they are wide ranging—one coyote's hunting range might be ten miles.

***A*bout 600 desert bighorn** *live in the mountains of Death Valley. A ram might weigh in at 180 pounds with a horn curl of 30 or more inches. Their varied diet— grasses, flowering plants, shrubs, and trees—is an adaptation to desert drought. They are threatened by people—by appropriation of water sources and by automobile disturbance in the backcountry.*

***S*idewinders are rattlesnakes.** *Small but quick, they loop gracefully and rapidly across the sand. This form of locomotion provides maximum traction in the loose sand, while at the same time keeping contact with the hot sand to a minimum. Mostly nocturnal, their prey is small rodents.*

***C*huckwallas take refuge in rock** *crevices, where they gulp air to make themselves bigger and wedge themselves in tight.*

The huge mountain blocks are broken,
ripped apart and tumbled.
Rock and mud are baked into a surreal landscape.
The valley floor is salt.
The word for Death Valley geology is "chaos."

The Record of the Rocks

MICHAEL COLLIER

Striped Butte is in *Warm Springs Canyon. Over 200 million years ago, when the Death Valley region was part of the Pacific Ocean's continental shelf, the striped limestone beds were deposited in horizontal layers. Since then, Death Valley's sedimentary layers have been tilted to every angle—Striped Butte is no exception.*

JEFF GNASS

Death Valley's geological history has three parts—all tumbled together: (1) Death Valley's rocks—the building blocks—vary in age from Precambrian times to the present. (2) Folding and faulting transformed the building blocks into "chaos." (3) Climate is a geological force shaping Death Valley.

THE BUILDING BLOCKS

The building blocks are tremendous accumulations of all kinds of rocks—sedimentary, metamorphic, and igneous.

The Hole in the Wall is a route into the *Funeral Mountains above Furnace Creek. Furnace Creek Wash is visible through the Hole, and, across Death Valley, Telescope Peak dominates the skyline. Most of Death Valley's sedimentary rocks date from the 300-million-year period (500-200 million years ago) when sediments several miles thick were being deposited in the shallow water of the continental shelf. Folding and faulting has since contorted them into every possible configuration.*

*F*or the last 9 million years or so, the Black Mountains have been tilting up to form Death Valley's southeastern rampart. During the uplift, sedimentary and volcanic layers have slid off the uptilting block. Black volcanic rocks are tumbled together with older sedimentary layers in a geological "chaos." The mountains are still rising—Death Valley is still happening.

TOM DANIELSEN

PRECAMBRIAN ERA (4,500-570 myBP [million years before present])—In Death Valley the oldest rocks are 1,800 million years old. Heat and pressure metamorphosed muds, sands, and volcanics into metamorphic schist and gneiss and, when the rocks were completely melted, granite. These oldest rocks form the dark colored "turtlebacks" along the Black Mountain front south of Badwater.

About 1,100 myBP, rocks of the Pahrump Group were laid down in a continental offshore shelf environment. Then molten lava was injected into layers of dolomite, metamorphosing it into talc and making possible 20th-century talc mining in southern Death Valley.

In latest Precambrian time, the conglomerate (mud, sand, and pebble) beds of the Kingston Peak Formation—exposed today in the Panamint Range—may be the record of an ancient ice age.

PALEOZOIC ERA (570-225 myBP)—Throughout Paleozoic time Death Valley remained part of a stable continental shelf on the edge of the Pacific Ocean. As new sediments were eroded off the land and deposited, the bedrock floor of the shelf sank deeper into the crust, making room for new sediments at the top.

In the Cambrian Period (570-500 myBP), muds and sands of the tidal flats were cemented into solid rock—sedimentary layers three miles thick.

Through the rest of Paleozoic time and into the Mesozoic Era, the Death Valley region lay further offshore. A two-mile thickness of carbonate rocks—limestones and dolomites (formed by algae, corals, and shellfish)—was deposited in warm, shallow, tropical seas.

In the Ordovician Period, about 450 myBP, a blanket of sand was deposited all the way from California to Alberta, Canada. In Death Valley this forms the Eureka Quartzite. The source of the sand is unknown. Otherwise, the carbonate deposition was uninterrupted for some 300 million years.

MESOZOIC ERA (225-65 myBP)—Rafted on subcrustal convection currents, the edge of the Pacific plate moved to the east and under North America. Friction and compression with depth caused melting. "Balloons" of molten magma melted their way toward the surface. Some of the granite plutons from the underthrusting of the Pacific plate are now exposed in Death Valley. Gold-bearing quartz veins associated with some of the granites are responsible for hardrock ore deposits at Skidoo, Harrisburg, and other sites.

In the Triassic Period (225-190 myBP), Death

Telescope Peak (11,049 feet) is the highest point within Death Valley National Park and the highest point of the Panamints, the block-faulted mountain range tilting up to form Death Valley's southwestern wall. These highest rocks are some 700 million years old—the younger layers have been stripped off.

Valley remained a shallow sea between volcanoes to the west and North America to the east. Shale and limestone from this time are exposed in Marble Canyon and to the south at Striped Butte. Thousands of feet of lava from the Sierra Nevada blanketed the Death Valley region.

CENOZOIC ERA (65 myBP-present)—River and lake sediments from 30-25 myBP form the Titus Canyon Formation. These colorful rocks in upper Titus Canyon and Titanothere Canyon are famous for their fossils of titanotheres (giant relatives of the rhinoceros), camels, deer, and tiny three-toed horses.

Volcanism has continued almost to the pre-sent. From 27 to 7 myBP, ash from tremendous and explosive volcanic eruptions in Nevada covered the Death Valley region. Some of the airborne ash flows were so hot that they welded together, forming welded tuff over a thousand feet thick.

Death Valley volcanism took place between 13 and 3.5 myBP, resulting in the lava flows of the Black Mountains and the Greenwater Range. Rhyolite lava, basalt lava, and ash flows are responsible for the colorful calico chaos of Artists Drive. Sporadic volcanism has continued almost to the present day. Ubehebe Crater and its dozen or so smaller companions erupted within the last 10,000 years.

The Furnace Creek Formation was deposited

Overleaf: The magnificent Eureka Sand Dunes in Eureka Valley are 680 feet high. As people walk down the dunes, the sand makes a moaning sound—the reason is unknown. The Eureka Dunes are part of the huge northwestern section of Death Valley National Park added in 1994 when the park was enlarged by 1.3 million acres. Photo by Marc Muench.

Fossils in sedimentary layers provide clues to ancient environments. These gastropods (snails) lived in shallow water on the continental shelf at the edge of the Pacific.

***T**he Grandstand is a granite outcrop in the middle of The Racetrack, a playa lake bed. The two received their names from this relationship—The Racetrack circling The Grandstand. The granite is about 100 million years old—formed when molten rock intruded the overlying layers from below and cooled into granite. In the intervening years the older layers were eroded away, exposing the granite at the surface.*

FRED HIRSCHMANN

from 9 to 5 myBP as muds in lakes and as gravels on alluvial fans above the lakes. In the dry climate birds, camels, cats, and even mastodons left tracks in the lakeshore muds. Today these form the yellow and brown badlands of Furnace Creek Wash—and contain the borax deposits.

Left undisturbed, all these intrusions, volcanics, and sedimentary layers would have formed a pile of rock several miles thick. What happened to them?

FOLDING AND FAULTING—AND CHAOS

Death Valley's rocks have been broken, uplifted, and downfaulted by two major and opposing episodes of faulting caused by crustal compression and then crustal extension.

COMPRESSION—The earth's crust was shortened.

The Death Valley rocks were folded and bro-

ken by regional compression. North America rode up and over the eastward-moving Pacific plate 200-150myBP. Along thrust faults many miles in extent, older layers were pushed to the east over younger layers. The earth's crust was shortened—compressed—by small amounts in some areas, by as much as 25 miles in others. Some of the layers—as in Titus Canyon—were folded upside down.

EXTENSION—The region was pulled apart.

Death Valley is part of the Basin and Range Province. Basins and ranges succeed one another in endless rows from California to Utah, and from Idaho south to Mexico. Death Valley is a basin surrounded by ranges. In 1874 the eminent geologist G. K. Gilbert correctly theorized that the basins and ranges had their origins in normal faulting, a process in which blocks of rock slide past one another in a predominantly vertical

Titus Canyon may be Death Valley's most scenic backcountry drive. The climax comes in the lower canyon—1,000-foot vertical walls, in places only the width of the road apart, block the sun. The walls are dolomite of the Paleozoic Bonanza King Formation—another continental shelf deposit laid down some 500 million years ago. About 150 million years ago the earth's crust here was compressed, possibly as much as 25 miles horizontally. Confined in a diminishing space, rock layers were broken and faulted and rolled over one another—in the Titus Canyon narrows the layers are upside down! More recently, as the Grapevine Mountains were tilted up, running water cut Titus Canyon.

direction. The upfaulted blocks form ranges; the downfaulted blocks form basins.

Death Valley's blocks are bounded by steep normal faults that flatten with depth. The faults are products of extension toward the east and west, a stretching of the earth's crust.

Basin and range faulting started about 12 myBP and continues to the present. The earth's crust was arched by magma (molten rock) intrusions at depth. The arching increased the area of the surface. The great building blocks, accumulated over 1,800 million years, broken and folded by Mesozoic thrust

faults, were broken again. To adjust to the greater surface area, great blocks of the earth's crust broke apart. In Death Valley, the blocks tilted up on the west and down to the east. The Panamint Mountains—Telescope Peak—tilted up to 11,049 feet. Badwater Basin tilted down about 9,000 feet below sea level. The deep basin is filled by debris washed off the mountains.

Basin and range faulting continues today. We can see fault scarps from recent earthquakes on the great alluvial fans. The fans on the east side of the valley remain much smaller than those on the west

side—the ongoing eastward tilting covers the toes of the east side fans with saltpan.

FURNACE CREEK FAULT ZONE—The Furnace Creek fault zone is a strike slip fault. Along the fault zone—from near Death Valley Junction to the Fish Lake Valley some 100 miles to the northwest—rocks along the west side of the fault have moved some 20 miles to the north, relative to the rocks on the east side. The most famous example of strike slip faulting is the San Andreas fault zone—California rocks on the west side of the fault are heading for Alaska!

CHAOS—The faulting was not "neat." Chaos replaced order. As the great mountain blocks tilted up, huge blocks and small blocks broke loose from the underlying backbone of solid Precambrian rocks and tumbled down the mountainsides—a few inches or a few tens of feet at a time. Many of the Paleozoic layers lie as broken blocks tilted against the mountainsides.

In the Black Mountains, as the Precambrian turtlebacks were tilted up, the younger layers slid off, exposing the ancient, somber-hued rocks on the range front. In the southern Black Mountains, in the area of Jubilee Pass and Salsberry Pass, geologists have named the cumulative effect of thousands of earthquakes the Amargosa Chaos!

Almost as fast as the mountains are uplifted, they are torn down. Water, mud, sand, trees, and boulders careen down the canyons in flash floods—and suddenly are disgorged onto the great alluvial fans. When the rushing water slows, it drops its load of debris and blocks its own path. When the next flood bursts out, it has to find a new path to the valley floor— and so the debris spreads out in the shape of a fan. Here, on the east side of the valley, continued tilting to the east buries the toes of the fans under the white saltpan.

The Pupfish Story

Pupfish are still here! They survived the evaporation of their world! In the last ice age, ending 10,000 years ago, they lived in lakes and rivers connecting the Sierra Nevada with the Colorado River. As their waters evaporated, they evolved into new species inhabiting desert waters—fresh and salt. Their ability to evolve with rapidly changing environments is incredible. Death Valley's pupfish live in the Ash Meadows, Nevada, detached section of the park, in Salt Creek, and in Saratoga Spring.

JEFF GNASS

More than 5 million years ago the Black Mountain and Greenwater Range volcanoes erupted and spewed out cubic miles of lava. As the Black Mountains were uplifted, blocks of the Artists Drive Formation slid off, forming another piece of the Death Valley geological chaos. Mineralized hot waters seeped through the rocks. At Artists Palette, iron minerals colored the rocks green and pink and orange.

"...the **younger layers** slid off, **exposing** the ancient... **rocks**"

Death Valley is the result of extreme basin and range faulting—a jigsaw puzzle gone crazy.

CLIMATE AS A GEOLOGICAL FORCE

Death Valley is the best example of the geological effects of the hottest place. In a more temperate climate, a more moist climate, a lake or river would cover the valley floor, feeding a river flowing out the south end to the Colorado River. In this desert climate, the valley floor is sinking faster than sediments washing off the mountains can fill it. Death Valley is a closed basin. A significant portion of the valley floor is below sea level.

Tens of thousands of years ago, in a colder and more moist climate, there was a 600-foot-deep lake in Death Valley—fed by Sierra Nevada meltwater. Pupfish made their way from the Colorado River to the Owens Valley and Mono Lake. Beach cliffs and gravel bars can be seen at Mormon Point on the Black Mountains and at Shoreline Butte. Lake Manly dried up 10,000 years ago, at the end of the last ice age.

Two thousand years ago, a 30-foot-deep lake covered the floor of Death Valley. When it evaporated, the Devils Golf Course—a layer of salt 3 to 5 feet thick—was left behind.

GEOLOGY STILL HAPPENS

Death Valley's rocks accumulated over 1.8 billion years. Over the last 12 million years, these rocks were broken into huge mountain blocks, the deepest valley, and chaos. Death Valley is the hottest and driest place—and this makes even the geology a little bit different. And the geology is still happening.

SUGGESTED READING

SHARP, ROBERT P., and ALLEN F. GLAZNER. *Geology Underfoot in Death Valley and Owens Valley*. Missoula, MT: Mountain Press Publishing Company, 1997.

Successive waves of people, beginning with Native Americans perhaps 7,000 years ago, have lived or passed through here and become Death Valley's history.

Those Who Came Before...

TOM BEAN

The Shoshone have lived in Death Valley for a thousand years. Few remnants of their old way of life are to be found. This petroglyph in Grapevine Canyon might be Shoshone, or it might be even older.

THE FIRST PEOPLE

Archaeologists have found traces of four distinct prehistoric cultures in Death Valley. The first of these people, known today only as the Nevares Spring culture, entered the valley about 7,000 years ago. More recent inhabitants were the Mesquite Flat culture (3000 B.C. to A.D. 1) and the Saratoga Springs culture (A.D. 1 to 1000). Ancestors of the present-day Shoshone entered Death Valley about A.D. 1000, eventually establishing their largest village at the mouth of what is now called Furnace Creek. According to early Anglo travelers in Death Valley, the Shoshone called their village Timbisha, meaning "Red Ochre."

The Shoshone living here adapted well to their harsh environment. Through the centuries they found sources for the water and raw materials needed to sustain life, and perfected hunting and gathering techniques. Even so, this valley did not support a very large Native American population. They lived in small kin groups, dividing their time between winter camps on the valley floor and summer camps in the mountains.

They lived in conical structures made of pole frames covered with brush. Much of their time was spent hunting and gathering food. Their staples were mesquite beans gathered on the valley floor and piñon nuts harvested in the mountains. Families banded together for rabbit or bighorn hunts and ceremonies. They manufactured tools and fashioned pottery and baskets to use in collecting and preserving their food.

Today members of the Timbisha Shoshone Tribe live on a small reservation at Furnace Creek in Death Valley.

THE '49ERS

The life of the Shoshone changed forever when the '49ers stumbled into Death Valley. They watched as people with huge wagons and immense oxen lost their way into the valley. They watched as the strangers—the first of the new people—staggered out.

Gold was discovered in California in 1848. The rush was on. Heading for the goldfields, a band of

Bound for the California goldfields, the '49ers stumbled into Death Valley, and out. They recorded their passing near Jayhawker Spring—modern petroglyphs.

In 1849 William Lewis Manly and John *Rogers hiked to Los Angeles and back— some 500 miles—to get help for the stranded emigrants in Death Valley. Manly Beacon, towering over the Furnace Creek badlands, was named to honor their courageous effort.*

'49ers left their guide to follow a shortcut. That shortcut cost them their wagons, their oxen, almost their lives. Looking for a way out, the '49ers fragmented into at least six smaller groups. William Manly and John Rogers left the Bennet-Arcan Party (the last names of two leaders) at Bennett's Long Camp on the valley floor and hiked 250 miles to Los Angeles to get help—and back again. After weeks of privation and suffering, a member of the Bennett-Arcan party, leaving the hottest and lowest place, looked back and muttered, "Goodbye, Death Valley!"—giving this place its name.

Later, Manly wrote:

It seemed the most God-forsaken country in the world. . . . One fellow said he knew this was the Creator's dumping ground where he had left the worthless dregs after making a world, and the devil had scraped them together a little.

One of the '49ers had picked up a piece of brightly colored metal in Death Valley. Later, in California, he asked a gunsmith to make it into a gunsight. The gunsmith recognized the metal as silver—and the legend of the "Lost Gunsight Lead" was born.

HARDROCK MINERS

In 1850 the first of the prospectors came, searching for the Lost Gunsight Lead. In 1860 a Christmas Day antimony strike became Death Valley's first producing mine, the "Christmas Gift." Jacob Breyfogle was found in 1864 on the Old Mormon Trail with gold-bearing quartz crystals in his pockets. He couldn't remember where he picked them up, and the legend of the "Lost Breyfogle Mine" was born. For 50 years thereafter,

prospectors went "breyfogling" in Death Valley.

1873—Panamint City—boom and bust—and then Chloride City, Keane Wonder, Bullfrog, Rhyolite, Skidoo, Ashford Mill—and the Leadfield swindle of 1926, where C. C. Julian proved that you didn't even need ore to sell mining stock—a few holes in the ground would suffice. There was always enough gold—or silver—to draw more prospectors, investors, and miners. The wealth poured into the rocks greatly exceeded the amount that was extracted.

WHITE GOLD

An exception to the history of mining failures in Death Valley is the story of borax. The "white gold of the desert" was mined profitably here from the 1880s to 1927.

In 1880 Aaron Winters found borax in Death Valley. The Eagle Borax Works started in 1881 and failed in 1884. From 1883 to 1887 Harmony Borax Works gave us the immortal 20-mule-teams that

RANDI HIRSCHMANN

hauled 36 1/2-ton loads 165 miles from Furnace Creek to the railhead at Mojave.

Then more successful mines were started in the east side mountains: Lila C., Biddy McCarthy, Grand View, and Widow. The Death Valley Railroad ran from Ryan to Death Valley Junction, where it met the Tonopah and Tidewater Railroad, which never reached either. When the T&T closed down the Beatty and Goldfield line, railroad ties were stacked in Tie Canyon to provide firewood for the 14 fire-places in Scotty's Castle.

Stephen T. Mather, a Chicago newspaper writer (more about him later) asked John R. Spears to write a romantic account of the California borax industry. In 1892 Spears wrote *Illustrated Sketches of Death Valley*, which included this account:

At last, the sun went down and the flaming color in the western sky faded and darkened until the shadows in the gorge of the Funeral Mountains where Winters was camped be-

came absolutely black. By the faint glow of a few dying coals Winters and his wife sat down on the sand, put a saucer of the material on the rock between them, poured the chemicals and alcohol over it, and then Winters scratched a match to fire the mixture. . . . Winters held the blaze to the mixture in the saucer with a trembling hand and then shouted at the top of his voice: "She burns green, Rosie! We're rich by——!"

At 25 cents a copy, Spears' *Illustrated Sketches* was a success. Mather was hired to be the Pacific Coast Borax Company's advertising and sales promotion manager. Mather created the "20 Mule Team Borax" logo to sell borax to America. Using dummy names, Mather wrote hundreds of letters

The Charcoal Kilns are in Wildrose
Canyon. From 1876 to 1879, Mexican laborers felled the piñon pine, fed the kilns to reduce the wood to charcoal, loaded wagons, and delivered the charcoal to the Modoc Mine silver smelter 25 miles to the west.

to newspapers extolling the virtues of borax. Then he published his own letters as *Borax: From the Desert, Through the Press, Into the Home: 200 Best Borax Recipes from More than 800 Issues of 250 Different Publications in 33 States of the Union.* The booklets were mailed with borax samples.

In 1897 Thomas Thorkildson founded the Stirling Borax Company. In 1903 Mather broke with the Pacific Coast Borax Company and joined Thorkildson. The two proceeded to make their fortunes.

DESERT RESORT AND PARK

The Shoshone and their predecessors lived in Death Valley for thousands of years. The '49ers were the forerunners of the prospectors who searched for treasure in every out-of-the-way peak and canyon—"boom-and-bust" gave the valley an adventuresome history. Borax and the 20-mule-teams provided another romantic chapter.

Richer borax deposits were found elsewhere and most borax mining in Death Valley ended in 1927. The Pacific Coast Borax Company retained its land and water holdings at Furnace Creek and constructed the Furnace Creek Inn as a resort, later offering additional accommodations at Furnace Creek Ranch. Intrepid tourists began to find their way and their numbers increased almost yearly. In 1933 Death Valley National Monument became part of our national park system. The Ranch and Inn continue to provide accommodations today.

Now Death Valley is a destination for those seeking to experience the nation's geographic and climatic extremes—and for those seeking more enduring values. They find treasure—not gold or silver—but the treasure within each of us that enables us to appreciate, cherish, and preserve.

STEPHEN T. MATHER

Steve Mather of the National Parks is must reading for all who love and enjoy the national parks. Author Robert Shankland tells the story of Mather's second life, begun when he was 47 years old, as the first director of the National Park Service.

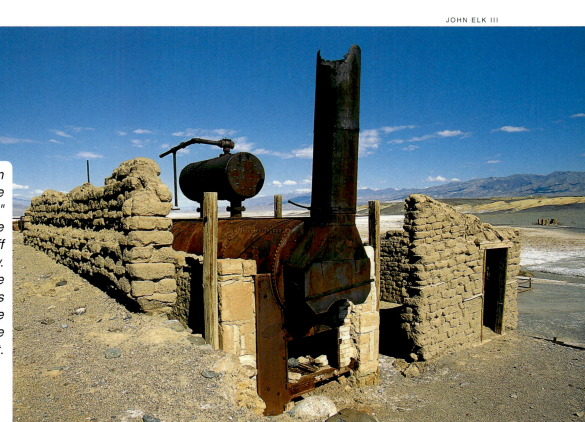

In the 1880s W. T. Coleman bought Aaron Winters' Death Valley claim for $20,000. He built and operated the Harmony Borax Works from 1883 until 1887. Chinese laborers scraped "cottonball" borax—so called because of its appearance—off the floor of Death Valley. Initial refining was done here to separate worthless mud and salt from the borax before the 20-mule-teams hauled it out.

The 20-mule-teams (actually 18 mules and 2 horses) hauled two wagons and a 1,200-gallon water tank—36 1/2 tons—out of Death Valley through Warm Springs Canyon and over Wingate Pass to the railhead at Mojave, 165 miles to the west—10 to 12 days one way. The muleskinner and his assistant, the swamper, each earned $75 to $120 a month.

Mather grew up in California and was an outdoorsman, mountaineer, and active member of the Sierra Club. He was personally acquainted with John Muir—the "father" of Yosemite National Park. Mather's work with the borax industry brought him face to face with Death Valley's fantastic desert—and Death Valley played an important part in preparing Mather for his role as "father" of the National Park Service.

In 1914 the nation possessed 13 national parks and 18 national monuments. They were administered—not very well—by the Agriculture, Interior, and War Departments. Mather, incensed at misuse and neglect of the parks, wrote an angry letter to Franklin K. Lane, Secretary of the Interior. Lane had known Mather 30 years earlier at the University of California. Lane wrote back,

The wagons cost W. T. Coleman $1,000 each —so well built that they lasted the five-year life of the 20-mule-team route from Harmony Borax Works to Mojave. Some are still intact today. Each wagon carried 12 tons of borax. In 1888 the Works was still profitable, but Coleman was overextended. In 1890, the bank sold his borax properties to Francis Marion ("Borax") Smith, founder of the Pacific Coast Borax Company. The 20-mule-team era was finished.

Dear Steve:

"If you **don't like** the **way** the national parks are being run, **come on down** to Washington and run them **yourself**"

Lane talked Mather into taking the job. Largely as a result of Mather's efforts, the National Park Service was established in 1916. Mather served as director until 1929. By then the parks had become an American institution.

Steam engines like #2—on display at the Borax Museum in Furnace Creek—carried borax from Ryan, in the eastern mountains of Death Valley, to Death Valley Junction, where it met the T&T, the Tonopah and Tidewater Railroad. The Death Valley Railroad operated from 1915 to 1927, when most borax mining in Death Valley came to an end.

-35-

Scotty and His Castle

Scotty's Castle is an Arabian Nights dream come true in northern Death Valley. Walter Scott, better known as "Death Valley Scotty," and Albert Johnson built the castle and lived the dream.

In his youth Scotty was a swamper on Death Valley's 20-mule-team wagons and traveled with Buffalo Bill Cody's Wild West Show. In 1905 he surfaced with gold from his fabulous mine in Death Valley and chartered a train for $5,000. The Coyote Special carried Scotty from Los Angeles to Chicago in the record time of 44 hours and 54 minutes.

By the 1920s, financier Albert Johnson had become Scotty's friend and benefactor. Together they built Scotty's Castle in Grapevine Canyon at a cost of $2 million.

Scotty often hinted that he had a gold mine hidden away in the remoteness of Death Valley—many believed him. Others said that Scotty's only real bonanza was his friendship with Johnson. Whatever the truth of the matter, Scotty earned his place as the most famous of Death Valley's legendary men—men whose tales (and sometimes their deeds) matched the scale of the valley.

TOM MYERS

Walter Scott, known to the world as Death Valley Scotty, was a 20-mule-team swamper, Wild West Show trick rider, miner, entrepreneur, and legend in his own time.

FRED HIRSCHMANN

On this plate, "J" stands for Scotty's friend Albert Johnson; "S" is for Scotty. "D.V.R." is for Death Valley Ranch, the proper name for Scotty's Castle.

FRED HIRSCHMANN

Scotty had his own bedroom on the first floor of the Castle. Photos and mementos from Scotty's days in show business line the walls. After the 20-mule-teams closed down in 1888, Scotty spent the next 12 years, off and on, as a stunt rider with the Wild West Show.

JEFF GNASS

***B**uilt in the Spanish Provincial mode,* the Castle was nine years building, and never completed. Work stopped in 1931. Scotty's Castle—more properly Death Valley Ranch—is an architectural masterpiece. It has to be to match the scale and grandeur of Death Valley. Albert Johnson, the financier behind the construction, always let Scotty stand in the spotlight—and Scotty claimed the Castle as his own. Visitors still marvel at the vision and imagination—and the meticulous architecture, landscaping, and interior décor. Albert Johnson died in 1948 at age 75. Scotty died in 1954 at age 81. He is buried at the Castle. In his will Johnson left the Castle to the Gospel Foundation of California. The Foundation maintained the Castle and conducted tours until 1970. In that year the National Park Service bought Scotty's Castle for $850,000 and it became an integral part of Death Valley National Monument. Since then, Death Valley Ranch has been maintained much as it was at the time of Johnson's death and the National Park Service conducts tours year round.*

JEFF GNASS

The Biggest National Park in the Lower 48

In 1994 the size of the park was increased by 1,300,000 acres—making it the largest national park in the lower 48 states. The park boundary was expanded to the north and west to include northern Death Valley, the Last Chance Range, the spectacular Eureka Dunes, and Panamint Springs. To the southeast, the Greenwater Range was added, and the Owlshead Mountains were added on the southwest. For the first time, all of Death Valley was included within the park, along with all of the mountain ranges that enclose it.

TOM GAMACHE

Death Valley is full of curiosities— *not all of them natural. Crankshaft Junction, on the Big Pine Road, is a match for Teakettle Junction on the way to The Racetrack.*

The Eureka Sand Dunes are perhaps the most *spectacular 1994 addition to the national park. Steady dune-building winds sweep the sand grains along the valley floor until an obstruction forces the wind to rise, or a widening of the valley saps the wind of its force. In either case, the sand is left behind.*

FRED HIRSCHMANN

Death Valley lies on the edge *of the Mojave Desert. Joshua trees (in background) are yuccas—as are the plants in the foreground—and are the identifying plant of the Mojave Desert. This stand is at Lee Flat, near Panamint Springs in one of the sections that were added to the park in 1994.*

FRED HIRSCHMANN

The Inyo Mountains *(part of the Inyo National Forest) overlook Salty Pond in the Saline Valley. Like Death Valley, Saline Valley has no outlet to the sea— salts washed out of the mountains find their way down to Salty Pond. Saline Valley was also added to Death Valley National Park in 1994.*

Many come to Death Valley for the first time to experience the "hottest" and the "lowest." They return, year after year, because Death Valley has enough variety to fill several lifetimes.

Being at Death Valley

JOHN ELK III

Mosaic Canyon is just a step away from the Stovepipe Wells Village resort. In Death Valley, wilderness is always just a step away. There are always more hiking opportunities—always new wilderness waiting to be explored. The valley is 150 miles long. The Panamint Range on Death Valley's west side and the Amargosa Range to the east are subdivided into six major mountain ranges. There is so much of Death Valley—intimate as in Mosaic Canyon, panoramic as at Aguereberry Point and Dantes View.

The Death Valley Museum in Furnace Creek opened in 1960—190 feet below sea
level. Attractive exhibits tell the story of Death Valley. Park rangers are on duty to help visitors make the most of their time in the park. Rangers also present interpretive programs and lead walks and hikes. Publications are available for purchase. The park headquarters is located in the same complex. The date palms in the patio behind the Museum provide a fine place for relaxing and birdwatching.

Death Valley has everything desert has to offer—and one thing more, Scotty's Castle. Tours through the Castle take place throughout the year, offering a unique experience in this unique desert. Tour guides tell of Scotty's unlikely life, the strange meeting of cowboy and financier, and the creativity and effort that produced their Death Valley Ranch.

Hikers reap rich rewards for their efforts. From the bristlecone and limber pines of the Panamint Range, the white saltpan, so far below, is another world away. One of Death Valley's many memorable hikes is the 3,000-foot climb from Mahogany Flat to the top of Telescope Peak.

Driving is a comfortable way to experience Death Valley. Twenty Mule Team Canyon Road winds through the badlands near Zabriskie Point. The park includes more than 3,000,000 acres of wilderness. But a network of roads—paved and primitive—provides access to almost all parts of the park.

TOM GAMACHE

Horseback riding is a way to see the valley at a more leisurely pace. Concessionaires rent horses and provide trail bosses to let you see the surroundings in tranquil harmony. This is a great way to enjoy the desert in the winter months.

TOM GAMACHE

Bicycles used to be a rarity in Death Valley—but no more. Bicycling here is exhilarating—especially on a ten mile run down into the valley. On the valley floor roads generally have gentle grades and good visibility. Here a cyclist experiences the contrast of the barren saltpan and the flowers of spring just a few feet above the salt.

"Death Valley encompasses more than 3 MILLION acres of wilderness"

SUGGESTED READING

BRYAN, T. SCOTT, and BETTY TUCKER-BRYAN. *The Explorer's Guide to Death Valley National Park*. Niwot: University of Colorado Press, 1995.

JOHNSON, BESSIE M. *Death Valley Scotty by Mabel*. Bishop, CA: Death Valley Natural History Assn., 1987.

JOHNSON, LEROY & JEAN. *Escape from Death Valley, As Told by William Lewis Manly and Other '49ers*. Reno: University of Nevada Press, 1987.

LAWSON, CLIFF. *A Traveler's Guide to Death Valley National Park*. Bishop, CA: Death Valley Natural History Assn., 1996.

LINGENFELTER, RICHARD E. *Death Valley & The Amargosa, A Land of Illusion*. Berkeley: University of California Press, 1986.

MITCHELL, ROGER. *Death Valley SUV Trails*. Oakhurst, CA: Track and Trail Publications, 2001.

PAHER, STANLEY W. *Death Valley's Scotty's Castle: The Story Behind the Scenery*. Las Vegas, NV: KC Publications, Inc., 1989.

SHANKLAND, ROBERT. *Steve Mather of the National Parks*. New York, NY: Alfred A. Knopf, 1951 (out of print).

WHEAT, FRANK. *California Desert Miracle, The Fight for Desert Parks and Wilderness*. El Cajon, CA: Sunbelt Publications, 1999.

ZDON, ANDY. *Desert Summits, A Climbing and Hiking Guide to California and Southern Nevada*. Bishop, CA: Spotted Dog Press, 2000.

TOM GAMACHE

Even Ubehebe Crater has a heavily traveled trail. The explosion crater is half a mile wide and 750 feet deep. Ubehebe and its dozen smaller companions erupted within the last few thousand years. The explosions occurred when molten rocks, melting their way toward the surface, came upon groundwater. The instant steam caused the explosive eruptions. The black layers at the top are ash and cinders ejected during the eruptions. Ubehebe is the youngest of the group of craters in northern Death Valley.

Death Valley Becomes a Park

In 1927 the Pacific Coast Borax Company discontinued mining in Death Valley. They retained their land and water rights, provided tourist accommodations at Furnace Creek Ranch, and constructed the Furnace Creek Inn. They invited Steve Mather, former borax executive and first director of the National Park Service, for a visit. Mather replied that Death Valley was of national park significance, but there was no chance of it becoming a national park because of his borax connections.

With Mather's death in 1930, the conflict of interest died. Most of the land already belonged to the federal government. Horace Albright, Steve Mather's successor as National Park Service director, worked to make Mather's dream of a national park area at Death Valley a reality. Finally, on February 11, 1933, President Herbert Hoover proclaimed Death Valley National Monument.

For decades thereafter, many who visited Death Valley and came to love it asked, "How come Death Valley is not a national park?" Its size, grandeur, and spectacular scenery were of national park quality. But prospectors roamed the mountains and roads were built to claims and mines. Feral burros damaged the fragile ecosystem.

The burros were removed in the 1980s. Thousands of mining claims were examined—almost all were found to be legally invalid.

And the citizens of California were becoming aroused to save the California deserts—the entire desert landscape from Interstate 15 to Nevada. Mining, motorcycles, off-road vehicles, and sheer numbers of people were damaging the dry lands. Desert tortoise and bighorn became symbols of the desert life-forms whose existence was threatened.

The Sierra Club pushed for desert protection. In 1984 the California Desert protection League was formed. The main thrust was for a new Mojave National Park. But Death Valley and Joshua Tree National Monument were both heavily impacted by mining claims, and both needed to be enlarged to protect their ecosystems and to provide topographic boundaries that made more sense.

Ten years of lobbying, debate, and attempts at compromise followed. Finally, in 1994, both houses of Congress passed the Desert Bill, and on October 31, President Bill Clinton signed it into law. The Mojave National Preserve and Joshua Tree National Park were established. And there was finally a Death Valley National Park. With the 1.3 million acres that the bill added to the park, Death Valley was now the largest national park in the lower 48 states.

Death Valley is badlands, saltpan, alluvial fan, mountain.

KATHLEEN NORRIS COOK

All About Death Valley

Death Valley Natural History Association

The Death Valley Natural History Association supports the park in many ways. A private, non-profit or-ganiza-tion, it was created to provide visitors with information to enhance their stay. Several sales outlets offer publications and other media about Death Valley; some of these books were published by the association. Proceeds from sales help fund yet other means of visitor enjoyment: the three-dimensional model of Death Valley on display in the Visitor Center and telescopes used by rangers in night sky programs.

CHUCKWALLA
PHOTO BY
BILL RATCLIFF

HOW TO CONTACT US:

Call us at
(760) 786-3200.

Write to us at:
Death Valley
National Park
P.O. Box 579
Death Valley, CA 92328

Visit our web site at:
www.nps.gov/deva

DEATHVALLEY Junior Ranger

Discover:

- *How many plants and animals you can see?*
  How have they adapted to the environment?

- *Is there any water in Death Valley?*
  Where is it and where does it go?

- *How many stars can you see at night?*

Pick up your Junior Ranger booklet from Furnace Creek Visitor Center, Stovepipe Wells Ranger Station, or Scotty's Castle, and let your journey begin.

Use your senses and explore Death Valley on a scavenger hunt, visit the many different places around the park like Devils Golf Course, Artists Drive, or tour Scotty's Castle. Visit with a ranger and complete the right number of activities for your age group, as well as a Special Project from the booklet.

Recite the Junior Ranger Pledge and you will be awarded the honorary Junior Ranger badge – wear it with pride!

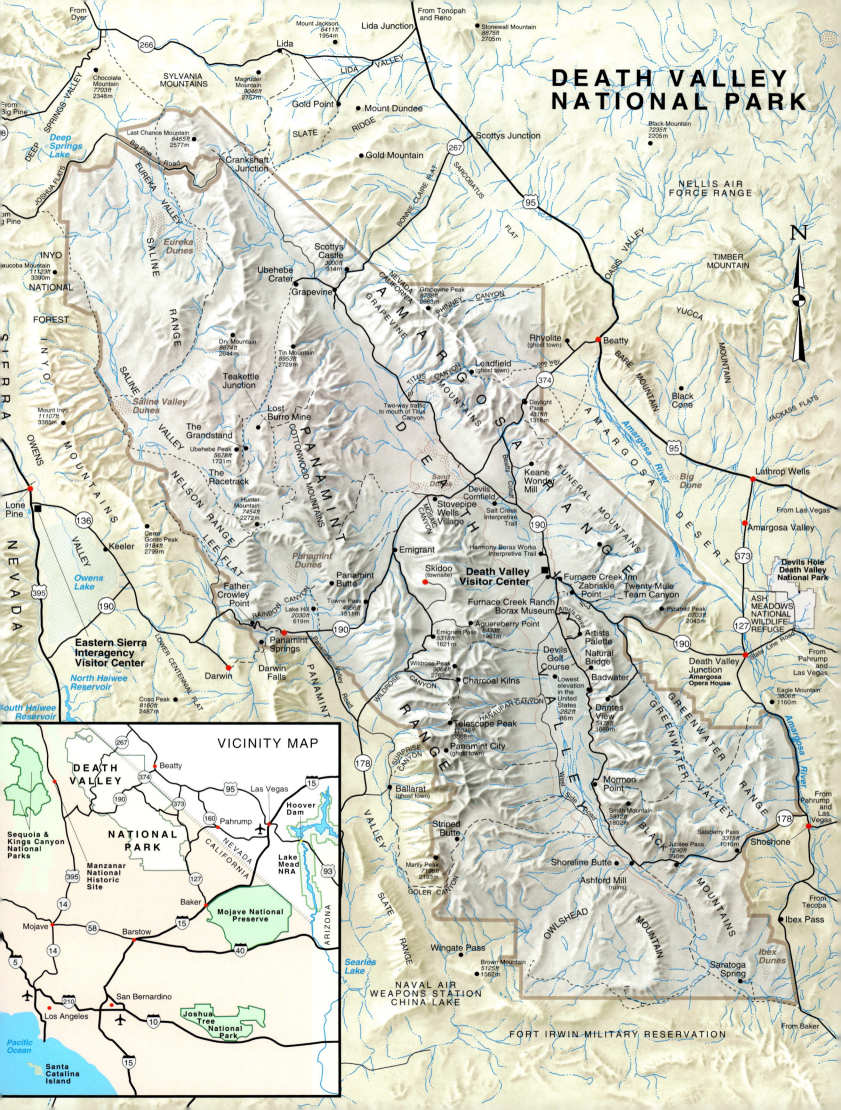

DEATH VALLEY NATIONAL PARK

N

VICINITY MAP

DEATH VALLEY

Beatty

Las Vegas

NATIONAL

PARK

Pahrump

Hoover Dam

Sequoia & Kings Canyon National Parks

Manzanar National Historic Site

Lake Mead NRA

Baker

Mojave National Preserve

Mojave

Barstow

Joshua Tree National Park

San Bernardino

Los Angeles

Pacific Ocean

Santa Catalina Island

A Look to the Future

Passage of the Desert Bill in 1994 seems to assure a secure future for Death Valley. Burros have been removed. The plethora of mining claims have been brought under control. The 1.3 million acres added to the park—for a total of 3.3 million acres—make its ecosystem whole.

Death Valley has always been a symbol of durability. Its mountain ramparts are contemptuous of human efforts to scar them. The saltpan is truly barren and lifeless, and throughout the park bad waters restrict human settlement to a few favored locations. The savage summer sun burns a warning to travelers. Yet the valley is enjoyed in all seasons by all kinds of people—some in armchairs in the campgrounds, others on endurance trials by foot or bicycle, and all of us in between.

Most of Death Valley is wilderness—forever free for us—forever free for the wild plants and animals who live here.

Badlands in Furnace Creek Wash contrast with snow on the Panamints.

JEFF GNASS

KC Publications has been the leading publisher of colorful, interpretive books about National Park areas, public lands, Indian lands, and related subjects for over 40 years. We have 6 active series—over 135 titles—with Translation Packages in up to 8 languages for over half the areas we cover. Write, call, or visit our web site for our full-color catalog.

Our series are:

The Story Behind the Scenery® – Compelling stories of over 65 National Park areas and similar Public Land areas. Some with Translation Packages.

in pictures... The Continuing Story® – A companion, pictorially oriented, series on America's National Parks. All titles have Translation Packages.

For Young Adventurers™ – Dedicated to young seekers and keepers of all things wild and sacred. Explore America's Heritage from A to Z.

Voyage of Discovery™ – Exploration of the expansion of the western United States.

Indian Culture and the Southwest – All about Native Americans, past and present.

Calendars – For National Parks in dramatic full color, and a companion Color Your Own series, with crayons.

To receive our full-color catalog featuring over 135 titles—Books, Calendars, Screen Scenes, Videos, Audio Tapes, and other related specialty products:

Call (800-626-9673), fax (702-433-3420), write to the address below, Or visit our web site at www.kcpublications.com

Published by KC Publications, 3245 E. Patrick Ln., Suite A, Las Vegas, NV 89120.

Inside back cover: *A skating rock at The Racetrack. (See page 12 for information about this phenomenon.) Photo by Fred Hirschmann.*

Back cover: *Scotty and his friend Albert Johnson lived their dream at Scotty's Castle. Photo by Fred Hirschmann.*

Created, Designed, and Published in the U.S.A.
Printed by Tien Wah Press (Pte.) Ltd, Singapore
Color Separations by United Graphic Pte. Ltd